THE

CHRONICLES

OF

Bizah

A

STUDENT OF TRUTH

THE

CHRONICLES

OF

A

STUDENT OF TRUTH

Constance Kellough

ILLUSTRATIONS · MARY KELLOUGH

books that change your life

namaste

PUBLISHING

VANCOUVER, CANADA

ISBN 978-1-897238-89-9 (Hardcover)

Library and Archives Canada Cataloguing in Publication
Title: The chronicles of Bizah: a student of truth / Constance Kellough ;
illustrations, Mary Kellough
Other titles: Bizah
Names: Kellough, Constance, 1947- author.
Description: Short stories
Identifiers: Canadiana 20200224298 | ISBN 9781897238899 (hardcover)
Classification: LCC PS8621.E4347 C47 2020 | DDC C813/.6—dc23

Published in Canada by Namaste Publishing Inc.
PO Box 72073
Vancouver BC, Canada V6R 4P2

Distributed by Ingram/Publisher's Group West

Cover and Interior Book Design: Mary Kellough

Printed on Recycled Paper in Canada by Friesens

To the Master of Truth Within All of Us.

While on a family vacation, Constance Kellough sat down to do some writing. Unexpectedly, a charming, playful, and wise character showed up – Bizah. The stories of his life with his Master and friends started to flow through her and on to the page.

She shared these stories in her meditation teachings, urging the participants when they listened to them to do so mindfully. They loved Bizah and quickly learned the lessons he had to teach them. In time, it became clear the world needed to meet him too.

*Please enjoy this collection of stories
in the silence of meditation, aloud in
gatherings, before or after yoga, or while
wrapped in a blanket at bedtime.*

*Let Bizah remind you of your own innate
truth – of the innocence, wisdom, and
goodness that exists inside all of us.*

*#WWBD?
When puzzled about what to do in a
particular situation, just ask yourself,
"What would Bizah do?"*

Contents

1   Bizah Doubts Himself

3   Washing the Master's Feet

6   To Give or Not to Give

9   The Companions

10   Just Round

12   On Red and Blue

13   Bizah Asks About Running

14   Bizah Goes for a Run

17   Bizah Feels Like He Is Being Run

18   Wondering About Worrying

21   Sharing a Story

22   The Arrival of the Student Prince

24   The Student Prince Humbles Bizah

26   Akina and Bizah Become Good Friends

29   The Master Has Only One Face

30   Bizah Gets a Pet. Bizah Looses His Pet

32   Bizah Decides Not to Replace His Lost Pet

35   Bizah's Next Pet Finds Him

36   Bizah's Cat Goes Missing

38   When You Come Up Against Unconsciousness

41   Nature As Our Teacher

42   Going Shopping

44   Bizah Makes a Hat

47   Bizah Learns to Listen to His Body

48   Incentive to Meditate

51   The Falsity Fear Brings

52   Noise

55   Tea for Two

56   Good-hearted Fool

59   Turn the Other Cheek

60	What Are You Looking For?
62	Two Hobblers
65	Vicarious Gift
66	Further Evidence of Oneness
68	Akina Becomes Manly
70	Labeling
73	On Eagles Flying High
74	Open to Receive, But Don't Forget to Also Send
76	Bizah Tries to Trick the Master
78	Bless You, Doggie
81	Bizah's Robe
82	Three Birds Cause a Disturbance
85	To Buy or Not to Buy?
86	Rainy Days
88	When to Answer a Plea for Help
90	Feed the Hungry
93	Bizah's Life Purpose
94	Golf Lessons
99	Bizah Makes His Bed
101	Blankets
102	Burdens Be Gone
105	Blithe Bird?
106	Peace Meets Anger
109	Bizah As Student
110	Bizah Questions His Reality
113	Humbug!
114	Bizah Dreams He Looses His Wallet
117	The Joy of Fishing
118	Bizah Learns the Right Use of Force
119	Already a Master
121	Bizah Makes Sponteneity Soup
122	Jugement Versus Fact
123	Signposts

125   Suffering

127   Bizah Gets Part Way There

129   The Gift of Presence

130   Bizah Learns the Importance of Surrendering to Life -
                    Whatever It Brings

133   Bizah Recognizes the Gift of Full Attention

134   Bizah Tells Tonga About the Body

136   The Plum Tree

139   Giving of Our Time to Others

140   The End of Waiting

141   Bizah Has Nightmares

143   The Greatest Gift

144   Eating Too Many Sweets

147   Tonga Impresses Bizah

148   A Long Day's Excursion

151   On Not Worrying About Others

152   On Understanding Angry Criticism

155   Service

156   The Myth of the Man in the Mask

159   Too Much of a Good Thing?

160   Bizah Learns About Gratitude

163   Bizah and the Thief

164   Watching Eagles Fly

167   Verbal Battling

168   Disguise is Disquieting After Awhile

171   When Work Is Too Hard

172   Giving And Receiving Part I

175   Giving And Receiving Part II - The Lesson Continues

179   On Saying "No" and Feeling Good About It

181   Bizah Continues to Learn About Giving and Receiving

182   If No Fish Bite?

185   Bizah and His Master

186   Life Interrupted

Bizah Doubts Himself

"Master," said Bizah, "I have been here studying with you with devotion and diligence for four long years. I don't think I have the kind of nature required to become a Master."

"Bizah," said the Master, "that belief is the only thing that is holding you back from replacing me as Master today."

Why limit your dreams and aspirations? They are free.

Washing the Master's Feet

Every day Bizah's love for his Master grew. He wondered how he could show his Master how much he honored him, how grateful he was for his counsel and presence in his life.

Then the answer came to him. "What better way to show the Master how much I honor him than to wash his feet!"

Bizah quickly dropped the book in his hand and ran over to the Master's abode. "Master, will you let me wash your feet?" he blurted out with enthusiasm.

"Why, of course, Bizah," the Master responded.

"I'll be right back." promised Bizah. "You just relax now, okay?"

Bizah ran to fetch a washing bowl, filled it with clean water, warmed the water on his little stove, took from his shelf the soap that had been given to him as a gift, then returned to the Master's house.

After Bizah gently and thoroughly washed both of the Master's feet, he dried them and carefully put the Master's sandals back on them.

"Bizah, I am so honored you wanted to wash my feet and that you were so present and diligent in doing so," said the Master. "Now, may I wash your feet?"

"What?" exclaimed Bizah. "I could never let you do that. You are the Master."

"Bizah, have I not taught you to serve and be served?"

"Yes, but…."

"Okay, now it is my turn to wash your feet."

The Master washed Bizah's feet with all the care and tenderness he could express through such an act. Bizah, though stunned and a little embarrassed, sat very still during the ritual.

"Finished," said the Master. "Now, how was that, Bizah?"

"Oh, could not have been better, Master," Bizah replied.

"Which did you prefer, your washing my feet or my washing yours?"

"Both equally, Master."

The Master's smile said it all.

To Give or Not to Give?

Bizah asked the Master a question he had been carrying for some time: "Master, should we give or not give to the poor?"

"Leela," the Master asked, "how would you answer this?"

"I always give what I can to the needy. I can't pass by one in need and not give if I still have a coin in my pocket."

"Tonga," the Master then asked, "how would you answer this question?"

"I don't give to those asking for alms. I think that maybe if I help, it will prevent them from finding ways to help themselves."

Bizah said, "Master, I asked you for your answer. I wasn't interested in hearing Leela's and Tonga's."

Said the Master, "It was necessary for you to hear their answers first, Bizah, before you could understand mine. Both Leela and Tonga were coming from a personal belief that dictated how they would respond to the poor they came upon. You can see from their answers that their beliefs are different and lead to conditioned responses.

"I never know whether I am going to give to the needy until I come upon them.   At that moment, I go inside myself and see how I feel about giving to that particular person at that particular time. I may give, or I may not give. But I will be acting from my own inner being, which is a much more reliable source for action than our conditioned beliefs."

What you give to others will
come back to you.

This is a law of life.

The Companions

It was a beautiful day, so Bizah asked Leela if she wanted to walk into town and have a cup of tea with him. Leela agreed joyfully.

As they were sipping their tea in the market square, Bizah saw two men sitting side by side against a brick wall. One wore a ragged blue jacket, the other a brown one.

The man wearing the blue jacket held out a small tin can for offerings; the man beside him sat with his hands resting on his lap and cupped open like a bowl.

A person came by and dropped a coin into the tin the man in the blue jacket was holding. When the donor moved on, the man took the coin from the can and gave it to his companion beside him, who accepted it gratefully, then cupped his hands again.

Bizah observed as this was repeated several times.

Finally, Bizah couldn't wait any longer. He just had to ask the man holding the tin can why he wanted alms but then gave the money away to the man beside him.

"Oh," the man in the blue jacket replied, "because my friend here is wanting for coins. I am wanting for love."

Just Round

Bizah hesitated for a moment, then he asked his best friend Tonga, "Do you think I am getting fat?"

"No, you are not fat, Bizah, just round."

"What do you mean, just round?"

"I mean you are round-looking."

"Does Leela think that too?"

"Yes, she says you are just round."

"Okay, today I am going to add exercise to my daily practices. Tonga, do you want to join me?"

"No."

"Why not?" asked Bizah.

"When I get round, I will join you then."

On Red and Blue

"Master," Bizah asked in earnest, "why is red, red? And why is blue, blue?"

"Wonderful question," responded the Master. "The answer is because you call red, red. And you call blue, blue."

Bizah Asks About Running

"Master, when I run, I don't know if I should just run until my body tells me to stop or to set some time and distance goals for myself each day."

"What do you want to do, Bizah?"

"Just run until my body tells me I have had enough that day."

"Then do that."

Bizah Goes for a Run

Bizah put his good robe to the side and donned a shorter white one. He was ready to get running.

The fifteen minutes were tough for him from start to finish. All he could do was think about not tripping , how much his knees hurt, and how his lungs burned.

When he got back he was met by his Master, who was smiling.

"Bizah, I hear that you are starting to exercise your body every day."

"Yes, but Master, I'm wondering if that is wise now. When I ran today, I wasn't mindful at all. All I could do was feel the aching in my body and watch out for stones so that I wouldn't trip over them. I didn't pay attention to the beauty of the trees or the sounds of the birds and insects. If I keep running, I will give up the greater portion – my contemplation of nature."

"Bizah, nature will still be there to contemplate after you have finished your run each day. And if you keep it up, there will come a time when you will not be running: you will be run. Then you can move quickly and also be still inside to not only take in the beauties of nature but also feel the beauty of your own magnificent form."

"But Master...."

"No excuses now, Bizah. This practice will be a very good one for you."

All change involves movement.

Bizah Feels Like He Is Being Run

"Master, you said that if I run long enough, I will come to the time when I feel I am being run. How is that?"

"Well, Bizah, you think the energy you use to run comes from yourself – from your legs, your lung power, your muscle power, your will – but it really comes from the inexhaustible supply of universal energy. If you run and run and run beyond what you think you can endure, you will have gone beyond your own energy output. When you are about to give up but don't, you will open to the energy that birthed and guides the universe. That energy is in you. It is inexhaustible."

"Now do you understand why I said that running would be a good practice for you?"

Wondering About Worrying

Bizah woke from a short and restless sleep. He was once again filled with worry – this time about a friend who suddenly took ill.

He got up to do some writing in his notebook. He wondered as he wrote why doing something – in this case writing about his day – helped to bring him ease when he got like this. He mused: why does worry thrive in idle times, in times of outward inaction? Why does worry like to visit during the middle of the night? Why is worry such a solitary activity that tends to leave when friends are around to talk to?

Just asking such questions seemed to distance worry, to bring Bizah ease.

Soon his pencil got heavy in his hand, and he went back to sleep.

Why is it when we hear a bird singing we usually think it is singing just for us?

Because it is!

Sharing a Story

There once was a village that was frequently visited by a beautiful white songbird. The bird appeared whenever someone needed to be reminded to drop sorrow and look at the things in their life to be grateful for.

Then one day the bird did not appear anymore. It had done its job. Because of its many previous visits, thanksgiving had become woven into the villagers' everyday life.

"Well, that's certainly a short and simple story, Bizah," said Tonga. "Is there any more to it?"

"No," replied Bizah. "A happy ending is a happy ending."

The Arrival of the Student Prince

A new student arrived to join the group. He was tall, eloquent, and walked with a distinctly regal mien. Although his name was Akina, Bizah started calling him "the student prince", certain that he came from some royal family.

Bizah also couldn't help but notice how much attention the new student got from the Master. "It isn't fair," thought Bizah. "Why should he get more attention than the rest of us, just because he is of royal blood?" he questioned. "The Master has never played favorites before."

Not being able to hold himself back any longer, Bizah approached his Master when the Master was alone and asked, "How come you are giving the new student so much attention? We have been studying with you a number of years now and you seem to have forgotten about us."

"Bizah," replied his Master, "Akina is new. He is having to make a lot of adjustments at this time. He needs a little more attention."

"But we need attention too," opined Bizah.

"Yes, I know," replied the Master. "Did you not hear my words, *a little more*?"

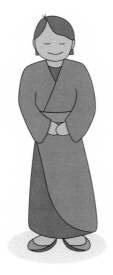

The Student Prince Humbles Bizah

The new student, Akina, who Bizah had mistaken for a prince because of his regal manner and the attention his Master gave him, had been with them now for several weeks. Bizah still didn't warm to him, thinking Akina must think himself better than others because of his royal blood.

Then one afternoon when Bizah was sitting outside playing with a homeless cat, Akina came by and asked Bizah if he could pet the cat. Bizah felt he had to agree, so he did so reluctantly.

Akina squatted down, picked up the cat, and stroked its back tenderly. When the cat began to purr, he purred along with him. Soon the cat fell asleep in Akina's arms.

"Well, you seem to really like cats and have a way with them," Bizah said.

"Yes, I love them. I had one for several years at the orphanage."

"The orphanage?" queried Bizah.

"Yes, I was orphaned when I was only two years old. My parents died in a fire."

Bizah was speechless.

"I thought you came from royal blood and your parents were influential and rich."

"Oh no, far from it. When my parents were alive they were poor farmers."

"But our Master treats you like you are someone special. Why is that?" asked Bizah.

"I don't know," replied Akina humbly.

The next day Bizah stopped his Master and told him about his encounter with Akina the day before, sharing what he had found out about him.

"Oh Master, I feel so sorry that I misjudged Akina. He is truly a warm and wonderful person."

The Master replied, "Well, Bizah, you have learned a lesson everyone needs to learn – and the sooner the better. Don't make assumptions about others. All you had to do was ask me about Akina, and I would have told you the facts."

Akina and Bizah Become Good Friends

Bizah could not stop thinking about how unfair he was to the newcomer Akina by making assumptions about him. He felt terrible.

"How could I have misjudged Akina as arrogant and aloof, when in truth he's gentle and humble?" he thought. "How could I have been so wrong? What can I do to make it up to him?"

The next day after lessons, Bizah asked Akina if he would like to go fishing with him in his little boat. Akina broke into a big smile and exclaimed, "Oh, I'd love to!"

As they sat fishing, they had ample time to talk. The more Akina talked, the more Bizah liked him.

Akina spoke of his friends at the orphanage with such love. He spoke of his caretakers there with such love too. And he expressed so much gratitude that when the Master heard he had such a special heart, he came to visit him then soon decided to take him on as one of his students.

"What I love most about the Master," said Akina, "is that he sees each one of his students as equally special and precious. He doesn't judge us. He only loves and instructs out of love."

Although Akina's words stung Bizah because they reminded him of how he had so terribly misjudged Akina, they also warmed his heart. He knew Akina would be a dear friend – and a special teacher too.

You cannot see and praise
in another what you do not
already have within yourself.

The Master Has Only One Face

With his heart full of gratitude, Bizah started extolling the virtues of his Master.

"Master, all of us studying with you are so fortunate to have such an exceptional Master. You are so wise, so kind, so patient, and compassionate. What a special Master you are!"

The Master took a moment before he responded.

"No, I'm not special. I am like any Master. We have the same face."

"And I'm like all of you too," the Master continued. "It is just that you have not seen the Master reflected back to you in your mirror yet."

Bizah Gets a Pet.
Bizah Loses His Pet

"Leela, Leela, look at my pet frog!" enthused Bizah.

"Oh, where did you get it?"

"I found him down by the pond sitting alone on a rock. When I went to pick him up, he didn't hop away. He just let me hold him and pat his back. I took this to mean he wanted to be my pet. I call him Greenie."

Six months passed with Greenie being Bizah's best ever, non-human friend. Everywhere Bizah went, you could find Greenie snuggled in his pocket.

Then one day Greenie disappeared. Bizah was bereft and couldn't be consoled by any of his friends. His Master heard about this and went to Bizah.

"Bizah, why are you so sad at having lost your pet frog? There are many other frogs down by the pond that you could have for a pet."

"But, Master, I don't want just any frog. I want my Greenie back. He is special to me. He is mine. We were great companions. I took such good care of him, and he never made any noises or jumped about when I had him in my pocket."

"Is Greenie really a special frog, Bizah, or did you make him special by giving him your attention and your care? Could it be that any frog would be special to you if you treated them the same way? Is it not by our loving someone or something that they become precious to us? Is it not by appreciating and caring for a pet that it becomes 'ours'. All of life responds to our appreciation of it, Bizah. Go down to the pond. Find another frog, give him a name, treat him like you did Greenie, and see if he too will be a fine pet."

Bizah Decides Not to Replace His Lost Pet

After losing his pet frog Greenie, even though the Master said he could make any other frog his pet too by treating it with the same love and care, Bizah could not do this. Regardless of what the Master said, his Greenie simply couldn't be replaced — at least for now.

Bizah felt he needed to honor Greenie by not replacing him so quickly with another frog. Indeed, he wondered if he would ever be able to do that.

He mused on this for several days, then came to see that just because the physical form of Greenie was gone, the place he took up in Bizah's heart was filled with the love he still had for him. No, there was no need to replace Greenie.

He really had not lost him.

Butterflies remind us to give
things the light touch.

Bizah's Next Pet Finds Him

Bizah's pet frog Greenie had been gone about a month when, as Bizah exited his abode, he almost stumbled over a small brown and white kitten. When he came home at the end of the day, the kitten was still there. Bizah tried to ignore her. He had no interest in having another pet. Greenie was still his pet, at heart.

The kitten stayed outside Bizah's abode for two more days, lying near his olive bush, watching him come and go. Bizah became concerned. Finally he gave in and fed the kitten some milk and mashed rice. The kitten's energy immediately picked up, and he started to purr and brush against Bizah's leg whenever he came near.

Bizah thought to himself, "What am I to do?"

He decided to relate the situation to his Master. The Master responded: "Bizah, you found Greenie on a rock by the pond and brought him home with you. You chose him as a pet. Well, this kitten has found you. He has chosen you to be his owner. Life has brought you this kitten for a reason. Take this kitten in, Bizah. Like it or not, he is yours."

Bizah's Cat Goes Missing

It was two nights now that Bizah's cat had stayed out and not come home. Twice before he had stayed away for one night, but never for two nights.

"Oh, no," cried Bizah. "What if he is lost? What if he has left me like my frog Greenie did? I just can't stand the pain of losing another pet."

The third night passed without a sign of Bizah's cat, so Bizah went to see his friend Akina to seek comfort. When Akina opened the door, there was his cat right beside him.

"What, you have my cat and didn't tell me?" exclaimed Bizah. "I have been worried sick that something awful had happened to him or that he had run away and wouldn't come back."

"Oh, Bizah, I thought you knew your cat must be over here. As you know, your cat and I have become good friends. Can't we share him?"

"But I'm the one he found, and I took him in," said Bizah.

"He's my pet."

"Bizah," said Akina, "your cat is showing you up. He can love two masters, but you insist on being the sole master of him. Who is showing the greater capacity to love? Your cat knows that sharing his love doesn't weaken the love he has for either you or me. Can we not learn to do as he does and share him between us, as well?"

When You Come Up Against Unconsciousness

"Master, you said that when I come up against human unconsciousness, to just observe it with compassion – that this is the only way to live in peace. But what if this unconsciousness is aggressively hurting me?"

"Can you give me an example, Bizah?" asked his Master.

"Well, what if someone is calling me mean and false names?"

"Do not take his name-calling personally," said the Master. "It has nothing to do with you. He is just projecting his own unhappiness, his sense of low self-worth, onto you. Let his name-calling just pass through you. Don't react to it. Observe and extend your compassion to him."

"Okay, Master. But what if he picks up a stick and is about to hit me with it?"

"Ah, that's a different matter. You need to personally protect yourself against this level of unconsciousness. You should grab the stick out of his hand, and with all the loving kindness in your heart – are you listening to this, Bizah? I said, 'With all the loving kindness in your heart,' give him one hard wake-up whack with it, enough to make him back away. Then throw the stick away."

"Have you ever had to do this, Master?" queried Bizah.

"Unfortunately, yes, Bizah."

Nature teaches us so many things if we let it - things like endurance, abundance, diversity, adaptation and resiliency.

Nature As Our Teacher

"Bizah, look at that mountain over there and see how the shaded areas reflect the clouds in the sky above. In this way, when we look at the mountain, we can also see the clouds," said Leela.

"Yes, I can see that, Leela," responded Bizah. "It's just like how the outer world reflects back to us something about ourselves. Like the Master said, 'As without, so within.'"

"And let's not forget 'as within, so without,'" added Leela. "Nature sure can remind us of principles of truth, if we are open to its language."

Going Shopping

Leela's birthday was coming up soon, and this year Bizah wanted to personalize her gift by actually making it with his own hands.

He went into town to see what materials he could buy. There were two shops that sold material and other sewing needs.

Bizah went into the first shop he came upon. Inside, the merchandise was well organized and appealing, much of it highly original. However, he found the sales people pushy and basically miserable - like many of their customers. Feeling the energy there repulsive, he left quickly.

Once outside, Bizah breathed a deep sigh of relief and walked on to the second handcrafts and material shop, stepping into this shop with some hesitancy.

To his surprise, Bizah found the atmosphere buoyant, with the sales people smiling warmly and engaging their customers in warm conversation. They weren't pushy at all.

The merchandise wasn't as well displayed, nor as original. But Bizah decided this was where he would make his purchase.

Back home, he related his experience to Tonga. "It was as if I entered two different worlds when I entered those two shops," he said. "How could that be, Tonga?"

"Well, you know why, Bizah," Tonga replied. "A person's attitude makes all the difference to the energy they give off and therefore the energy they attract. This becomes even more evident when a group of people with the same attitude gather together – like in those shops."

Bizah Makes a Hat

With Leela's birthday still approaching, Bizah decided to make her a hat with the help of a pattern he bought at the materials and sewing needs store.

He left himself plenty of time to complete the project: two weeks. When he told Akina what he was planning for Leela's gift, Akina asked, "Bizah, have you ever sewn anything from a pattern before?"

"Actually no," responded Bizah.

"Bizah, for goodness sake, why did you start with a hat?" asked Akina. "Didn't you know that a hat is one of the most difficult things to make?"

"Really?" responded Bizah. "But a hat is so small."

At that response, all Akina could do was wave a gentle "good luck" goodbye.

Two weeks later at Leela's birthday party, Bizah proudly presented her with his gift. It was wrapped in magenta satin material and tied with a magenta ribbon.

Leela received the package from Bizah with both arms and hands outstretched, as if she were receiving the crown jewels. Opening her gift slowly and respectfully, she uttered a gasp of both surprise and delight.

Removing the hat from the wrapping, she placed it on her head. "Oh, Bizah, this is the most beautiful hat I have ever seen!" she exclaimed.

"And so becoming on you, Leela," said Bizah, feeling quite puffed up because he had such an eye for style.

"Oh, look," exclaimed Leela, "you even embroidered my name inside it."

"That's because I don't want you to lose it, Leela. It's a one and only."

Bizah's gift was the talk of the party. His friends approached him to ask if he would make them hats, as well.

Bizah kept shaking his head. When the requests persisted, he felt he was forced to make his point emphatically. "Didn't you hear what I told Leela? That hat is a one and only."

Just then, Akina caught Bizah's eye and gave him a knowing giggle.

Silence is the language in
which the Divine speaks to us.

Bizah Learns to Listen to His Body

Bizah and the other students were eating lunch with their Master at the communal table.

"Master," Bizah piped up, "how do we know the best things to eat for good health? And how do we know how much of anything to eat?"

The Master responded, "Listen to your body. Its needs change from day to day. Become sensitive to what your body wants you to feed it at any one time. If you pay attention to your body, it will also tell you when you have had enough to eat."

"Thank you, Master," said Bizah.

Soon after, Bizah pushed his half-empty plate away. "My body does not want very much rice today."

"Oh, thank you, Bizah," said his Master as he took Bizah's plate. "Mine does."

Incentive to Meditate

The Master began speaking. "When you spontaneously laugh, are you thinking?" he asked.

"No," Leela responded.

"When you experience deep peace, are you thinking?" the Master asked.

"No," replied Akina.

"When you are overtaken with love for someone, are you thinking?" the Master asked.

"No," responded Tonga.

"When you are in a state of awe, are you thinking?" the Master asked.

"No," Bizah said.

The Master then fell silent and his students joined him in meditation.

We can never understand the whole from bits of our perception, which is all we can see. This is another reason to refrain from judgement.

The Falsity Fear Brings

Bizah shared a story with Tonga. There was a father who sent his daughter down to the river to fetch water for tea.

As the father waited for the daughter to return, a neighbor ran in and said that someone had just been found dead in the river.

"Oh, no," the man moaned. Then he broke into tears. Soon after, he became hysterical. "My one and only daughter; I have lost her. And it is all my fault. I was the one who sent her to the river to fetch water. Oh, what will I do now? How can I go on?"

Just then the daughter entered through the doorway holding a full pail of water. "What is wrong, father?" she blurted out.

"Oh, our neighbor came in and said they found someone dead in the river, and I just assumed it was you. It wasn't though. Oh, I am so relieved, so happy."

"Dearest father," asked the daughter "why didn't you go down to the river and see for yourself who drowned? Then you would have been dealing with fact, not assumption. You could have saved yourself that acute anxiety and sorrow. You let your fear lead you to make an assumption. You placed your faith in fear, not in fact."

"Good one," Tonga said to Bizah.

Noise

Bizah headed out to a festival day in the village. The festival was to celebrate the life of one of their leaders who had recently died. Although Bizah didn't really know who this person was or what he had done to serve the villagers in such important ways, he decided to go for the camaraderie, color, and fun that would predictably surround the festivities.

As he headed out, the road was packed with people shuffling along while loudly chattering to anyone who would listen. Children were crying for attention, parents were grumbling, and dogs were barking. As people were about to enter the village, there were large, flapping flags staked into the ground to welcome them.

The festivities were at their peak. Sellers were yelling out, declaring the value of their wares and produce to anyone who came near. The product stalls were made blazingly colorful in order to attract potential buyers. Varied, loud, and mainly frenzied music, some of it even discordant, came at Bizah from all angles. People were dancing wildly, frenetically – not joyously.

Bizah made his escape into a shop he presumed would be relatively quiet because it sold magazines, only to discover that these also, with their bright colors and exaggerated images, "shouted" at him. Even they were "noisy".

After finding something to eat, Bizah headed back home. Because he left the festival so early, there were few who moved along the road with him.

"I went to experience some camaraderie and levity amongst the town folks," thought Bizah, "and found only noise. No doubt my quiet life studying with our Master has made me more sensitive to noise. Thank goodness."

Is there anything after
surrendering to what is?

Yes, the knowing that all is
well, because there is no place
that love is not.

Tea for Two

"Hi, Bizah!" greeted Akina. "Fancy meeting you now, because I'm just heading to your house to ask you to join me for tea."

"No kidding." Bizah replied with surprise. "Why, I was just heading to your place to ask you to do the same thing. Funny how we both were prompted to invite each other to tea at the same time."

"Well, we have become very close friends, Bizah, and do share with each other at a very deep level. Because of this, we are really not separate in our consciousness anymore."

"I guess you are right, Akina. Okay, let's try this: where would I prefer to have tea with you? At your place or mine?"

Akina became still for a moment then responded, "At my place."

"Right!" exclaimed Bizah. "Now, how did you guess that?"

"Because I have the best biscuits," replied Akina.

Good-hearted Fool

"Master, I heard the other day of a man in the next village who sold his donkey to a poor farmer for four bags of rice. Then a week later he bought it back from the farmer for six bags of rice. What a foolish man."

"Not necessarily," responded the Master. "What do they say of this man who sold, then bought back his donkey?"

"Well, Master, they say he is a good man with a very kind and generous heart. But from this donkey incident, I can tell he sure isn't very smart."

"Can you think of any reason why he would have sold, then bought back the donkey for two more bags of rice then he sold it for initially, Bizah?"

"No, I can't. It doesn't make sense."

"Not to your mind. But now start thinking with your heart."

Bizah sat down and pondered the situation again, this time from his heart. Of course, now he understood clearly.

"Oh, Master, how could I not have seen that the man sold the donkey and bought it back for more than he sold it because it was a way of giving to the poor farmer without making it seem like the farmer was receiving charity. And in doing this, he made the poor farmer look like a good business man and himself like a fool."

"Yes, Bizah, what they say about this man is true," said the Master. "He does have a very kind and generous heart. And his heart is also very wise."

By assuming the role of the "witness", you are not avoiding external reality, just acquiring a truer perception of it.

Turn the Other Cheek

Akina was throwing rocks into the lake, when for no reason a bully came up to him and pushed him to the ground.

Akina got up. The bully, wanting to get a reaction from Akina, pushed him to the ground again.

Once again Akina got up but said and did nothing. The bully pushed him down once more and with more force this time.

Akina got up once again and just stood there, looking into the eyes of the bully.

After a moment, the bully turned his back on Akina and walked away, mouthing a sound that expressed his disgust.

Bizah then ran up to Akina. "I have been watching all this time. Why did you let that bully keep shoving you down for no reason? Don't you feel humiliated?"

"Not at all," replied Akina. "I just held to what the Master said is the true strength of a man. He could push my body down but could not touch my being.

"It's odd but true, Bizah. By not asserting myself in this situation, I feel like I am the one who is stronger."

What Are You Looking For?

Bizah and Akina took two days of vacation together. They went down to the seaside to enjoy the ocean air, the vista, the warmth, and the sand.

On their first day, as they looked out at the vast ocean, they saw an old man walking back and forth along the sand. He looked out to the ocean, up at the sky, down at the sand, to his right, to his left, then behind him. This continued for some time.

Bizah got concerned.

"Akina, I think that old man has lost something. It must be important because he is searching so earnestly and continuously. Let's go see if we can help him find it."

Bizah and Akina ran to meet the old man.

"Old man," said Bizah, "we have been watching you for some time now. You have been searching desperately for something you lost. Can we help you find it?"

"Looking for?" asked the man with astonishment. "I haven't lost anything."

"Then why do you keep looking to the sky, the ocean, the sand, to your right and to your left and behind you all the time?" questioned Bizah.

"Oh, that's just a habit of mine. I keep searching for something of value in the world, but still haven't found it. As you can see, I'm old and now wonder if I will find it before I die."

Bizah was about to respond to the old man, then stopped himself.

Bidding the old man adieu, Bizah and Akina went back to their sitting area.

"Oh, Akina," Bizah said. "Isn't it sad that old man has spent most of his life searching for something of value outside of himself when thanks to our Master, we, at such a young age, already know all that is of true value must first be found within us."

Two Hobblers

Bizah, being a wonderful observer of people and of life, related a story to Tonga one day.

"There were two very old men walking toward each other from opposite directions along a trail. Both hobbled along tentatively, relying heavily on support from their canes.

"One of the hobblers came to a fallen tree along his part of the path. He tried to step over it but looked like he was going to fall attempting to do so.

"The hobbler coming from the other direction saw this and speeded up to go help prevent the other old man from falling.

"When he reached him and made his attempt, he too was about to fall but was helped by his fellow hobbler. It was quite a site to see both decrepit men hanging onto each other while trying to come to the other's aid.

"Eventually, they both stabilized and decided to avoid the fallen tree altogether by walking around it. Soon they both were on their way again, hobbling in opposite directions."

"I swear, Tonga," said Bizah, "when they both started on their own way again, they were walking with more strength, confidence, and stability."

It was just as the Master said: "We find our strength in service to others."

It's your choice as to whether you see tragedy as a punishment or a challenge.

Vicarious Gift

It was the second day of their vacation at the seaside. Both Bizah and Akina had quickly become lost in the delicious stillness, rarely speaking but observant and highly alert.

For a long time now, Bizah had been watching a partly crippled man limp along the sand holding a cane while his black Labrador ran in and out of the water, splashing and jumping happily at play.

After the dog ventured into the water to play for a few minutes, he would return each time to his owner and lick his free hand.

From the man's unbridled laughter and the expression on his face, Bizah felt the man's delight at his dog's happiness made the man forget he couldn't romp and play that way himself.

Further Evidence of Oneness

Bizah got up suddenly and headed to Akina's, not knowing why. When he arrived, he found Akina sitting on the floor nursing his bleeding knee.

"Goodness, what happened, Akina?" Bizah asked.

"Oh, I wasn't looking and tripped over a fallen tree branch on my way home and scraped my knee badly," replied Akina. "But why are you here now? I didn't expect to see you here?"

"That's a good question," Bizah responded. "I really don't know, other than that I was just sitting quietly at home, then my body got up, and I knew I had to come see you."

"Hmm," replied Akina. "More evidence that we are becoming very attuned to one another. You sensed something was wrong with me and just came."

"I guess so," said Bizah. "But how does that really happen – that we become so attuned we can sense what is happening to each other?"

"Well, we sure spend a lot of time in stillness together. During these times, we experience an inner presence, which is not personal, but universal. It is in all things. So as we cultivate this inner presence, we must become closer."

"Why?" asked Bizah.

"Because there is not your presence and my presence, there is simply presence. We are in truth all one, and our spiritual practice is bringing us into this realization through our experiences."

"Awesome!" exclaimed Bizah. "Should we tell the Master?"

"I think he already knows this," replied Akina.

Akina Becomes Manly

One day Bizah observed something that surprised him: Akina was starting to grow a beard. Now that he thought about it, it seemed like his voice was starting to deepen as well. "Goodness," thought Bizah, "Akina is starting to become a man already!"

"But why him first?" he questioned. "I am six months older than him."

For some reason – that being sheer envy – Bizah started becoming somewhat distant from Akina. He didn't initiate invitations for tea any more and kept his conversations with Akina quite short and to the point.

Akina could not understand Bizah's changed behavior, his aloofness, his remoteness. Whenever he tried to get close to Bizah, he was not so subtly rebuffed.

After a month or so, Bizah noticed he too now was growing a beard. He ran over to Akina's as soon as he saw this, threw his arms around him, and gave him a warm bear hug.

"Well, what is the cause for all of this sudden affection?" queried Akina with surprise in his voice.

"Look. Look, Akina. I am growing a beard now just like you!" Bizah exclaimed.

"Is that what this has all been about, Bizah? You were envious because I started to show signs of manhood first?"

"I guess so," replied Bizah. "We were so close; then you started to change, to show signs of maturing before I did – and I am 6 months older."

"Bizah, how can you be so shallow? How can you let something like that interfere with our friendship?" asked Akina.

Bizah started to tear up. He couldn't speak, just turned around and left.

Labeling

"Master, here are some wild flowers I picked for you."

"Thank you, Bizah."

"I can't remember their names, though."

"Their names do not matter. Names are simply labels to put on flowers so the mind will feel comfortable 'knowing' the flower. You don't need to name a flower or know the name of it to experience its essence – its ethereal quality, its beauty, its ambrosial fragrance."

"But Master," Bizah replied, "I have a name, Tonga has a name, you have a name. A person has to have a name, or how else could you identify them?"

"That's true, Bizah. For practical purposes, we do need to have a name. But without knowing your name, you would still be who you are to me – a loving soul reaching to claim more of its own light."

Shine enough light on a flaw
and it becomes beautiful.

On Eagles and Flying High

Bizah one day asked, "Why is the eagle able to fly so high, Master?"

"To the eagle, he does not fly high. He just flies," responded the Master.

Open to Receive, But Don't Forget to Also Send

"Tonga, I had an awareness yesterday when I was meditating," said Bizah.

"Oh?" replied Tonga.

"Yes, you know how the Master says that when we sit in stillness it is a perfect time to open to receive from the field of All That Is, that we should listen to what the universal field of consciousness has to say to us, to give to us?"

"Yes."

"And that we should listen very carefully, be open like grateful receivers?"

"Yes."

Well, yesterday, I was listening for the vibration of peace. I wanted to be the receiver of peace. I waited and listened, waited and listened. Then, I had an insight: why don't I first send peace to the infinite field so it can send it back to me?"

"And that's what I did," continued Bizah.

"I went into my feeling body and sent you peace, I sent Leela and Akina and the Master peace. It felt good. And today I feel such deep delicious peace.

"The Master told about one side of this meditation, not the other."

"Bizah, I am sure the Master knew about the other side too, but wanted one of us to discover this for ourselves," said Tonga.

"I wouldn't be too sure of that," Bizah piped back. "Let's go to the Master and check this out."

Bizah Tries to Trick the Master

"Okay, Tonga," said Bizah, "now it's my turn to tell a story. There was a village in which those who lied grew long teeth. In time, the rest of the villagers learned how to outsmart them. Whenever they encountered a person with long teeth, they would tell them a lie, so that when the long-toothed liar shared the information, he would in fact be telling the truth. Following me so far, Tonga?"

"Barely."

"This continued for many years. During that time a boy was born who naturally grew long teeth, but was very honest. One day, there was a fire in one of the village huts. The elder who lived in that hut ran to get help. The first person he encountered was the honest boy with long teeth.

"Seeing the fright in the elder's eyes, the boy asked, 'What's wrong?'

"The elder screamed out, 'My house has been flooded! Run and get help!'

"The honest, long-toothed boy ran to the center of the village and screamed out the news for all to hear and come to the elder's aids. Seeing his teeth, the other villagers believed he must be lying: the elder's hut was not flooded but on fire."

"Tonga, you look lost."

"I am."

"Good. I want to have some fun with the Master. I am going to tell him this story then ask him what the lesson is."

With Tonga at his heels, Bizah set out for the Master's abode. He shared the story with the Master, then in a mischievous tone asked, "Oh, Master, can you tell us what lesson this story teaches?"

"Hmmm," said the Master as he fingered his chin and dropped into silence. A few moments later he responded, "The lesson is that water will not put out a flood."

"You're right! Very good, Master!" Bizah exclaimed.

Bless You, Doggie

"Akina, you know how much I love animals, especially dogs," said Bizah. "Well, the other day I was walking in the woods and met a man with his aged dog. The dog was limping and struggling along the path very slowly. I could see from all the lumps on his body that he was not well and likely suffering significantly. I stopped and said, 'Your dog looks like he is quite old, sir.'

"'Yes,' responded the man. 'He is almost 15 years old. He is not well, and this is his last walk.'

"It took a moment for what the dog's owner had said to sink in. When it did, my heart instantly went out to both of them – that brave dog who held on to life in spite of his suffering because he loved his master so, and the owner who I could see was already distraught in anticipation of the loss of his beloved pet.

"I leaned down to pet the dog and at the same time gave him my silent blessing. Before I continued on my way, I turned to the man and said, 'It is very hard. Bless you.'

"He looked at me with tears in his eyes and gave a slight nod. As I started to walk away, I recalled how the Master told us that blessing others, aloud or in silence, is a powerful way of extending our heart and healing energy. But I also realized we can use the power of blessing for animals too. And why not plants, and rocks, and...."

When you look at a situation and say, "Nothing has changed, yet everything has changed", remember that something HAS changed - you!

Bizah's Robe

One day, when climbing down a tree, Bizah tore a big hole in his robe. So he quickly took it to the town's tailor to have it mended.

While he was without his robe, Bizah noticed that people were not as kind or courteous to him, even though he was still the same Bizah.

"How can people suddenly change their view of you when you change your clothes?" Bizah asked his Master.

"I know, it does not make sense," his Master responded.

A few days later, Bizah had his robe back. When his Master saw him he asked, "How do you feel now that you are able to wear your robe again?"

"Oh, I feel wonderful."

"Hmm," said the Master, "that doesn't make sense to me either, Bizah."

Three Birds Cause a Disturbance

"Master," Bizah began, "yesterday I had extra bread that was getting too dry to eat, so I broke it into pieces and put it outside for the birds. Well, you can imagine that in no time at all, one bird flew down to feast on a piece. He ate his fill and flew away.

"Then a second bird came and started eating. He had just begun nibbling away when a third and bigger bird flew down and aggressively pecked at him to go away and leave the rest for him. The second bird quickly flew away."

"Why are you telling me this story, Bizah?" asked the Master.

"It was so disturbing to see that kind of aggression and greed, even in the animal kingdom, where I know most behavior is dictated by survival instinct," said Bizah sadly.

"And knowing this is how it is, why then did you find it so disturbing?"

"Well," responded Bizah, "I guess it's because I see this happening among humans as well. When there is plenty for all, some are aggressive and greedy, wanting everything for themselves. I just can't understand this."

"Ah, yes, that is really what is bothering you," replied the Master.

"Bizah, consciousness cannot understand unconsciousness with the mind," the Master went on to explain. "It can only recognize it. When you encounter human unconsciousness, just observe it with compassion. This is the only way to live in peace."

The nature of a polished diamond is to sparkle. It needs nothing outside of itself in order to do this. The same applies to all of us.

To Buy or Not to Buy?

"Akina," Bizah said, "I saw the most beautiful blue vase in a shop the other day. The shape of it was like nothing I have seen before – a combination of a swan and a tulip, I would say. The various shades of blue just melted into one another in a way that made the whole vase seem iridescent.

"If I bought it, it would bring me pleasure each time my eyes fell upon it. But then again, it is so expensive and doesn't at all go with the other things I have in my room."

"Bizah," inquired Akina, "why are you telling me about this?"

"Well, I guess because I want you to help me decide whether I should buy the vase or not," replied Bizah.

"If you need me to help you decide this, Bizah, then you are not ready to buy the vase."

"Thanks, Akina."

Rainy Days

"What is it about rainy days that make us feel less lively and a bit sad?" Bizah asked himself as he slumped lethargically into his favorite chair.

"Is it because the rain can prevent us from doing pleasant outdoor things like going shopping or for a walk?

"Is it because most people stay home and don't visit you when it rains?

"Is it because rain evokes memories of contrasting happier times?

"Is it because the flowers don't seem as colorful in the rain?

"Is it because the falling rain reminds us of our unshed tears?

"All of the above," thought Bizah as he pulled his soft comfort blanket on himself and purposely sank his body deeper into the chair.

When To Answer a Plea for Help

"Give me food, I am hungry."

"Let me enter, I am homeless."

"Please visit me, I am lonely."

"There are so many, many people in need. How can I determine who to help?" Bizah asked himself. After posing the question, he let it float off.

That night Bizah had a dream. He found himself under a big oak tree with one hand outstretched and full of bread. The birds overhead were many and all hungry. They swooped down in droves to grab the bread from his outstretched hand. In no time, the food was gone. However, birds continued to fly towards Bizah to see if there was a morsel left for them, becoming aggressive when they found no bread at all.

Bizah's hand was scratched and bloody. It hurt so much that he put it in his pocket in order to protect it. His other hand, which had been empty of any bread, hung freely from his arm.

"What a curious dream," Bizah said to himself upon waking.

"Does it mean I must realize I can only help so many in

need before my helping turns on me and weakens me? Or does it mean I should help others when it comes easily for me and therefore I am able to continue to be of service?"

After posing these questions, once again Bizah just let them float off. That night he had another dream....

Feed the Hungry

Bizah had a serial dream. He always paid special attention to his serial dreams because they cautioned him about things he was not yet conscious of.

Almost every week for the past two months, Bizah had dreamed he had many, many hungry guests in his home and needed to feed them. There were so many guests, but only him to do the work.

He washed all the vegetables, prepared the meat and the sauces, took down the plates, but no matter how hard he worked, he never got enough food onto the table to feed his guests. He worked and worked and worked, but it was never enough. He simply could not feed such a crowd. Each morning he awakened from this dream feeling exhausted and sad.

Then suddenly, the serial dream took on another aspect. Now he found himself in the same situation, but with helpers in the kitchen. It was still challenging just overseeing and giving directions to the kitchen helpers, but they did manage to get the meal onto the table to feed the guests. No sooner had they accomplished this, however, than it was time to prepare for the next meal of the day.

When Bizah awoke from his dream the next morning, he was less exhausted, but frustrated.

The following week, his dream took a dramatic turn. He found himself sitting at the table eating with his guests, while others were waiting on them. The food was the finest and the conversation most congenial and inspiring.

When Bizah awoke the next morning he felt refreshed and full of joy. "What a change in this dream!" he exclaimed. "What could have caused such a dramatic and positive shift? What do I need to learn from this?"

Once again, Bizah just posed his questions, then let them float off, confident the answers would come.

Two days later an answer did come.

Bizah had been thinking it was up to him to do everything he could for others. His sense of personal responsibility for others was unhealthy for him, draining him.

It was suddenly obvious to Bizah that those in need will always be there, but when we give up our efforting and struggling, and let the Presence within us do the work, more are taken care of, including ourselves. Then service is joyful and replenishing.

Upon this realization, Bizah thought to himself, "It's just as the Master said: "The universal one Presence within us does the work for us – and AS us."

We would do better if we knew
a better way of doing things.

Awareness changes
everything.

Bizah's Life Purpose

"Master, when will I know that I have achieved my life purpose?" asked Bizah.

An unusually long silence passed between the Master and Bizah.

Then, slowly and with emphasis on each word, the Master responded, "When the notion of your life purpose no longer holds any meaning."

Golf Lessons

Bizah shared with his friends a story he heard in town:

In the town two miles down the road, the youth became very problematic. Having too much time on their hands, they got into trouble at every turn.

The elders got together and decided this problem would require the wisdom of a Master. The invitation went out.

Upon the Master's arrival, he quickly assessed the situation. He then asked that all the youth meet him in the open field at the end of town at noon the next day.

"I am going to teach you golf," he told them when they arrived, then went on at length, explaining the game and its rules to them.

"But we don't have any room to play golf," a boy with blazing red hair piped up. Another added laughingly, "Yes, we barely have room for one hole in this field, let alone 18."

"Don't worry," replied the Master. "You only need one hole to learn the game of golf."

He then directed the youth to map out a par 4 hole. For some reason, the boys especially liked digging out the two large bunkers.

Bringing in and stamping down the grassy turf for the green was the hardest part. By the time the flagpole was ready to be put in the hole, there was a faint sense of achievement growing amongst the youth. Appropriately, they gave the honor of this achievement to the Master.

"Now," he said, "here are three golf clubs: one to first hit the ball as far as you can, then one to hit it until it gets on to the green, and one to putt the ball into the hole."

The most brazen of the girls stepped forward. "Oh, come now, Master, how can we all play this one hole with only 3 clubs?"

"It's not so difficult if you take turns and learn from watching each other. Watch how each player holds the clubs, how he stands, when his swing works for him and when it doesn't. I will only step in and coach you if you ask for my help.

"And there is only one rule to my game of golf: You must each make three pars in a row and in succession. Then you may go and do whatever you like."

A weak-looking girl piped up. "That's not fair. Why do we all have to make three pars in a row in succession in order for any one of us to complete this training?"

"That's my rule," responded the Master emphatically.

"And you promised to teach us the game of golf. How can we learn to play golf if we only have one hole to play over and over again instead of the 18 on a full course?"

The Master simply responded, "As I said, you only need one hole to learn the game of golf. "

Months passed. The youth met at noon each day and often weren't dismissed until dusk.

Then one day, it happened!! All of them in succession scored a par. Cheers were heard throughout the town. The jubilant youth were so loud that the town folk came running to find out the cause for such a celebration.

As the youth headed home from the golf area that day, their heads were high and their postures erect.

Three more months passed. The youth practiced their game of golf each day until the miracle happened! All made 3 pars in a row.

This time, there were not cheers, no jumping up and down, no hitting on the back to congratulate each other – just a pervasive silence. Then, together, as if one body, the youth turned with gratitude to face the Master.

The Master put his hands together in "Namaste" and gave a slow and honoring bow to all of them.

Tom, the natural leader who emerged from the group, broke the silence by speaking for all when he asked, "How can we ever thank you, Master?"

"Gather yourselves together tonight, speak about what you have all learned from this little game of golf; then, meet me here again at noon tomorrow to share this with me."

The next day the group arrived at the appointed time and place, each one carrying flowers for the Master. With a simple hand signal from him, they all sat down.

"Proceed," said the Master.

Tom stood up, took a paper from his pocket and began to read the comments.

"I learned that you don't have to have competition to do your best."

"That if you do something well once, you can do it again and again just as well."

"I learned how to observe others and myself, and by this

means, how to self-correct."

"I learned that if I got down on myself, my game never improved."

"That you cannot play a perfect game until you learn how to play a perfect hole."

"How to have patience when others still need to learn something you personally have already mastered."

"I learned to want for others what I wanted for myself."

" We could do the seemingly impossible."

"No one wins unless we all win."

"Perseverance pays off."

"I learned ...."

Bizah Makes His Bed

One morning, Bizah went to his Master to admit he had just discovered he had been making up his bed incorrectly for the last four years.

"Oh, don't worry about it, Bizah," said the Master. "That way was the way to do it then. This is the way to do it now. You have been a student long enough to learn the better way. This makes me happy."

True friends are like warm blankets.
They are comforting to have
around us.

Blankets

"Tonga, listen to the poem I made up," said Bizah:

"What need have we of blankets?

"More than any precious gems:
They keep us warm in winter,
And protect us from the rain.

"They are a friend, a comforter,
So cozy and so soft.
What would we do without one?
We truly would be lost."

"Bizah, what inspired you to write a poem about blankets,
of all things?" asked Tonga.

"I gave mine away yesterday to a homeless person."

Burdens Be Gone

As was his wont, the Master started his lesson with a story:

"There was a worn and grouchy woman who daily walked through the village square. She could always be seen dragging along heavy bags of potatoes, one in each hand. She had a thick metal belt around her waist, and on her head she balanced a basket of stones.

"One day a visitor arrived in the square. Upon seeing her for the first time, he went up to her with the most intense curiosity and asked: 'Why are you carrying that useless basket of stones on your head?'

"'What? Stones?' the woman queried. 'Really?'

"She then flicked her head to one side and the basket with stones fell to the ground. To her surprise she felt a sudden relief all through her head, neck, and shoulders.

"'And why are you dragging those old rotten potatoes around?' the visitor asked next.

"'What? Rotten potatoes?' the woman responded in horror, then looked down at her hands to see the two sacks she had been dragging along.

"'Oh,' said the woman, 'I surely do not need these,' then immediately released her grip on them. She walked on, leaving the potatoes behind. How much lighter and younger she now felt!

"'And gosh, woman, look at that heavy metal belt you have around your waist. It is really unattractive.'

"The woman looked down at her waist and had to agree with the visitor that it really was quite ugly. With her hands now free, she unclasped the buckle and threw the belt in a nearby bush.

"Now, burden-free, she walked upright and happily along."

After a short pause, the Master asked, "What was the woman's real problem? Her burdens or her unawareness of them?"

"Oh," responded Bizah immediately, "that's easy. It was her unawareness of them. As soon as she became aware of them, she tossed them away."

"Yes," agreed the Master, "awareness brings correction. That's why we seek it."

Speculation is a way of keeping the mind busy, but it doesn't get you anywhere.

Blithe Bird?

"Tonga, look at that bird," said Bizah. "He has been sitting on the same branch in the same place all morning. He must be very pleased and content where he is."

"Maybe not," responded Tonga. "Perhaps he is injured and can't fly."

"Hmmm," replied Bizah. "Perhaps he is waiting for his mate to return and find him there."

"Could be. But what if the bird is just afraid to fly and try out its wings over new terrains?"

"Or maybe it just likes to sit in that particular type of tree," mused Bizah.

"Bizah, let's stop all this speculating and just enjoy looking at the beautiful bird," said the Master who was standing by and overheard the conversation.

"But Master...."

"No excuses now, Bizah. This is another very good practice for you."

Peace Meets Anger

Bizah was once again entertaining his friends with a story, this time an allegorical one. "One day, Peace was out walking in the garden, taking in the exhilarating smells and sights of nature, when she happened upon Anger.

"Anger raced through the garden tearing at flowers and pulling up bushes. Anger pushed over the fountain and chopped away at the bench under the still oak tree."

"'Why are you doing this?' asked Peace.

"'Because I want to be alone. I want everyone to hate me, to run from me. I feel powerful and protected when I am alone with myself.'

"'Oh, that's very strange,' said Peace. 'Well, I'm not upset by you, Anger. I will stay with you no matter what. You can destroy this garden and all the gardens on the planet, and I will still stay with you.'

"'Don't do that, Peace. Please don't do that,' replied Anger. 'I will have no strength if you keep accepting me no matter what I do. I will become weak and will have to give into your gentle ways.'

"'Well, that's precisely what I exact of you for all of your foolishness,' said Peace.

"The end," said Bizah.

Tonga turned to Leela and said, "Good story. That Bizah sure knows how to keep us coming back."

A true spiritual Master knows
they will always be a student.

Bizah as Student

After spending eight years with his Master learning all he could from him, Bizah could not restrain himself any longer. He had to ask his Master the question he had dwelled on constantly of late.

"Master, have you found me to be a good student?"

"You are neither a good student nor a bad student," said the Master. "You are just a student. And when you become a Master, you will be neither a good Master nor a bad Master. You will just be a Master."

Bizah Questions His Reality

"Master," Bizah said one day. "Some say that everything we see is just an illusion. That all is really illusion. If this is so, how do I know that I am not an illusion, just dreaming that I am Bizah?"

"Oh, yes," replied the Master. "I have heard this many times too. You are not ready to go too deeply into this yet, but I will ask you – do you feel you are real?"

"Why, yes, of course. I'm here talking to you now, aren't I?"

"Fine, but how do you know you are real? Close your eyes. Do you see yourself here with me now?"

"No, I can't see myself, because my eyes are closed."

"Then how do you know you are here?"

"Because even though my eyes are closed and I can't see myself, I can feel myself here."

"Very good," replied the Master. "Are you aware of the feeling of the life energy inside you?"

"Yes."

"Then who is the one who is aware?"

"I am!" exclaimed Bizah.

"Well, there you go," said the Master. "Now, why don't you join the others at play."

@BizahSays

Chaos brings with it great
opportunities for creativity.
Everything is in upheaval and
therefore can be rearranged,
easily changed.

Humbug!

"Tonga," said Bizah, "it's that time of year again when everyone goes a little mad, running around trying to get their homes in order, decorate them, invite people over for festivities, frantically looking for the perfect gifts for their family and friends. I just want to opt out of all of this craziness this year. Humbug to Mid-winter festival."

"I know, it can get a bit much, Bizah," Tonga replied. "But what would winter be without it?"

Bizah fell into silence.

Bizah Dreams He Loses His Wallet

"Master, Master!" called Bizah. "Please help me interpret a dream I had last night.

"I was walking along a path in the woods and for some reason took out my wallet and put it on a log. I continued on my way. When I was almost out of the woods, I remembered that I left my wallet behind and started to panic. I wanted desperately to go back and get it but I couldn't because it was now dark and if I did, I would get lost. Now, what was that all about?"

"Bizah, why were you afraid when you realized you left your wallet behind?" asked the Master.

"Well, because it has all of my identification in it. If I lost it, how would I be able to prove to people who I am?"

"Bizah, I think your dream means that you know you need to leave your old identity behind and grow into a new one, but you are afraid to do so. It's a good sign that you did not go back and get it – even if you didn't go out of fear. Your Inner Knower is telling you that you are growing out of your old identity into a new one. That's good news."

@BizahSays

If we have no expectations,
we open ourselves to being
pleasantly surprised.

The Joy of Fishing

"Akina, why do we enjoy fishing so much?" asked Bizah.

"It's relaxing. All we have to do is put our rod in the water and wait for the fish to come to us. And if a fish doesn't bite, we still had fun anticipating it would."

"Hmm, I wish we could do this with life in general," said Bizah.

"Why can't we?" Akina responded.

Bizah Learns the Right Use of Force

"Master," Bizah asked, "is there ever a time when it is okay to use force against another?"

"This is a good question, Bizah," said the Master. "Let me tell you a story. Before you came to be with me, I had a group of three students who were very serious and studied extremely hard. One day, I told them they needed to have some fun and suggested they go into the village and take in the sights and sounds at the market.

"Because the village was several miles away, they decided to take a rickshaw.

"That evening after supper, they started to tell me about their afternoon. The female student couldn't wait to tell me how disappointed she was that, because of something that happened, she didn't have any money to bring me back a little present.

"She explained, 'Just when we were getting into the rickshaw, Master, a gang of young men came running by, and one of them stopped and tried to wrestle my purse from me. I struggled and struggled with him for almost a minute, but in the end, his strength was too much, and he ran away with my purse.'

"'Oh, my dear,' I said. 'As soon as the thief went for your purse, with only his best interests at heart, why didn't you hit him over the head with your umbrella?'"

Already a Master

"Oh, Master, I wish I could already be enlightened like you!" exclaimed Bizah.

The Master smiled then responded, "You already are, Bizah. You just won't allow yourself to accept this."

When we experience chance occurrences, serendipitous events, incredible coincidences, let's remember that they didn't just happen to us - we co-created them.

Bizah Makes Spontaneity Soup

It became a custom that every Friday Bizah prepared his Master a special soup. Several days in advance, Bizah planned what kind of soup he would make, then took a special trip to the market to purchase fresh ingredients.

Friday rolled around again, and at the appointed hour, Bizah carefully walked the hot bowl of soup over to his Master. Then he stood back, watching closely to see how his Master would react to the soup.

The Master took a sip and smiled. He took another sip and smiled even more broadly. Then he paused, looked at Bizah, and said, "Bizah, this is the finest soup you have ever served me."

"Really?" Bizah said with surprise. "This time I didn't use a recipe, just whatever I felt should go in it."

"Ah, I thought so," said his Master. "That is always when you can make the best soup."

Jugement Versus Fact

Bizah and his Master would go to the village once a week to have a special kind of tea at a small restaurant.

On one such occasion, Bizah said, "Look over there, Master. That man is very selfish and uncaring. He has eaten all the food and left his wife with none."

"Bizah, remember you should not judge others," said his Master.

The next week when they went to the village for their teatime, the same man and his wife were there again. Once more, the man ate all the food.

The Master said, "Look at that man, Bizah. He has eaten all the food."

"Master," Bizah said, "last week you told me not to judge others and now you do so yourself. I am confused."

Said the Master: "Two weeks ago, what you said was a judgment, Bizah. What I said today was not a judgment: it was a fact."

Signposts

Bizah's Master ended his teaching that day as he had done before on other days. He said, "Remember that even though I am the Master, I cannot teach you the Truth. That you must come to on your own through your own felt confirming awareness or direct experiences. I can only point you to the treasure; you must be the one to go and find it. I can only give you signposts, pointers to the Truth. And even these signposts are of no use to you unless you continue to follow in the direction they point you."

All his students could do was continue to look at him with admiring eyes and nod.

Life is not a bowl of cherries,
it's the bowl - and we fill it with
whatever we choose.

Suffering

"Master," said Bizah, "it pains me so to see humanity in all of its suffering. What can I do to relieve it?"

There was a long silence before the Master responded, "Do not dwell on the suffering, but the reality of love and joy all around you."

Bizah Gets Part Way There

"Okay, students," the Master said. "Today I have another quiz for you. What is the closest thing to you at this time?"

"This desk," said Tonga.

"This pen," said Baton.

"The ring I am wearing," said Leela.

"No, none of you are correct," responded the Master.

"Hmmm," said Leela. "Could it be our hands and feet?"

"Very good, Leela," said the Master. "You are getting close."

"Master, there is nothing closer to us than our hands and feet," said Bizah.

"Oh?" questioned the Master. "Close your eyes and sit in stillness now."

Five, ten, then fifteen minutes passed.

Suddenly, Bizah jumped up and yelled, "I know, I know, Master! It's the sensation in our body!"

"You've got it!" said his Master smiling broadly. "That is one of the reasons we practice sitting in stillness and silence. When you want to be the closest you can to your life essence, go into your body and feel it. Once you can do this, you are part way there."

"Part way where?" asked Leela.

"That's enough for today," responded the Master as he slowly walked away.

Silence is not quiet.

It is wisdom's loudest voice.

The Gift of Presence

Bizah related a recent experience to Akina. "I was sitting on a rock by the river when an old man came hobbling along. For no reason at all, he stopped to talk to me. I could tell he was very lonely, since he couldn't wait to pour out his life story. I just sat and listened.

"When he finally finished talking, he bowed low, expressed his deep gratitude, and left giving me his blessing.

"Akina, I don't understand why he was so grateful. I didn't even say anything to him. I didn't even give him one piece of advice, which you know I'm prone to doing when given the opportunity."

"Bizah," responded Akina, "you gave that old man something very precious: you gave him your presence. You listened deeply to him, as if he were the only man in the world and his story the only story ever told."

Bizah Learns the Importance of Surrendering to Life – Whatever It Brings

"Master," asked Bizah, "what does it mean to surrender to life?"

"What would you do if you were given a beautiful bowl as a gift?" replied his Master.

"Why, accept it, of course," said Bizah.

"And if you were given an invitation to a wedding party?"

" Accept that too."

"And if you broke your leg?"

"I guess once it was broken," said Bizah reluctantly, "I would have to accept it and try to make the best of it."

"Would you accept it in the same way you did the gift and the invitation?"

"Well, no. I happily accepted the bowl and the invitation. I would sadly accept my broken leg."

"Bizah, 'surrender' is when you can just as happily accept your broken leg as you accepted the gift and the invitation."

"But Master, that seems almost impossible to do. It would be unfortunate that I broke my leg."

"How do you know that, Bizah?" his Master queried. "When you come to understand that life is FOR us at all times, and that it can only be benign and loving, you will surrender to everything – and then you will come to see that everything is a gift."

If we truly understood that
we are all one, we would
generously give only good
things to others, knowing that
whatever we give we simply
give back to ourselves.

Bizah Recognizes The Gift of Full Attention

"Master," said Bizah, "when I go to the market every other week, there is one fruit merchant who is always so much busier than the others, even though he sells the same fruit. Is there a reason so many more buy from him?"

"Well, Bizah, do you also buy your fruit from him instead of from the other fruit merchants?" asked the Master.

"Yes."

"Why?"

"Because he is always so friendly and present with me – even when I buy just one piece of fruit. So I go away feeling good."

"You have just answered your own question, Bizah. This merchant is giving you more than the fruit you buy. He is giving you that something extra, that something special – his full attention and appreciation. Some call this 'Presence'."

Bizah Tells Tonga About the Body

Bizah and Tonga had finished with their schooling and chores for the day, so they decided to sit down by the lake.

Tonga was the first to break the silence.

"Bizah," he said, "my sister just lost her husband and is in the deepest grief imaginable. She is in anguish night and day. She says she doesn't want to be here anymore, doesn't want to go on living alone without her husband."

"Oh, your sister has not yet accepted that just the body of her husband has died," Bizah explained. "She is resisting the fact his body has gone. If she keeps resisting this fact, she will not be able to accept the grief of loss and go through her mourning."

"And once she accepts that her husband's body is no longer here with her, she will be able to open herself to the essence of her husband as something that can never die?" asked Tonga.

"She will have him with her always," said Bizah. "She will still be able to be one with him in her spirit. And spirit is so much more animated, joyful, fulfilling, and expansive than what we can experience with another in the body."

Tonga looked puzzled. "Why is that?"

"Because the density of the body seems to restrict how high two people can soar together," said Bizah. "Without the body, there is no limit to the expansion and expression of their love."

The Plum Tree

"When will I be ready to be of real service to others, Master?" asked Bizah.

"Look at that plum tree, Bizah," replied the Master. "It is not yet ready to produce plums. It knows that for now, it needs to take in nourishment from the air, the ground, the sun. Then in the right season and at the right time, it will be able to produce many plums for others."

@BizahSays

You can't create when you are
thinking about the past or the
future.

You create your life in the
Now.

Giving of Our Time to Others

One afternoon Bizah started thinking again about giving to others.

"Why is it so hard to give of our time to others? We can't run out of it. There's always a now moment to give our attention to, so always a now moment in which we can give our attention to others. If this is so – and it is – why aren't we more present with others in our life?"

As Bizah continued in this inquiry, he concluded that the reason we are so greedy of our own time is that we are rarely in the only real time there is: the present moment.

When we don't abide in the present moment, but are away most of the time visiting the past or future in our mind, we become deluded into thinking we don't have enough time. "How silly we humans are," he thought.

The End of Waiting

Tonga was late again. How many times in the past few weeks was he to meet Bizah at an agreed upon time to go down to the pond for a swim, only to make Bizah wait and wait for him. It's not that Bizah didn't tell Tonga every time he was late that he got frustrated at having to wait and impressed upon him the importance of keeping his time commitments.

Bizah sat on the nearest rock and started to examine the situation more deeply.

Point number one: Tonga is persistently late. Point number two: this frustrates me and makes me angry. Point number three: Tonga shows no indication that he is going to change his habit of arriving late for his appointments.

"Okay," mused Bizah. "It seems that Tonga is not going to change his behavior, in which case I will continue to get frustrated and resent him for it. Hey, this is really not about Tonga at all: it's about me! Tonga is free to be late, and I am free to go to the pond ahead of him."

Bizah Has Nightmares

"Master, I am not sleeping well at night again. I get tired and fall asleep for a few hours, then awaken after a jarring nightmare. These nightmares are different, yet the same. They all relate to a former friend who betrayed me. I thought I had gotten over this ages ago, but I guess I haven't."

"Sometimes, Bizah, we don't allow ourselves to feel our painful emotions deeply and fully. We suppress them. They then reside in the subconscious awaiting a time to surface and be released. Such a time is often when our defenses are down during our sleep. This kind of dream you are now experiencing is very healing. Your subconscious is trying to rid itself of your remaining pain. When it does, you will experience greater wholeness and freedom. Now, Bizah, if you have another of these dreams tonight, what will you do?"

"I will look at it, feel the accompanying emotions fully – no matter how unpleasant they are – then let them go."

"Anything else?"

"I will be grateful that I am being healed of past emotional pain."

"Yes, and when you no longer have such dreams, you will know the healing is complete."

@BizahSays

When it comes to growing in
spiritual awareness, you can't
skip steps - but others who
have gone the way before you
can certainly teach you how to
accelerate your speed.

The Greatest Gift

"Master," Bizah queried, "what is the greatest gift you can give someone?"

Said the Master, "The greatest gift you can give to another is yourself. To give yourself to another means that when you are together, you are fully present with them and truly listen to them with every cell in your body – without judging them, their situation, or whatever they are saying."

"But Master," Bizah responded, "often when I tell you something, you tell me I have got it wrong."

"That's not judgment," Bizah. "That's fact."

Eating Too Many Sweets

"Master, why don't you ever tell us stories about when you were young like us? What were your adventures, your delights, your challenges? Who were your friends and what were they like?"

"Bizah, I don't go to the past these days unless I need to do so. I find that I have all I need right now, here in the present moment, to teach you what I have learned."

"This is very good to know, Master," Leela piped up, "but please, can't you search your memory and come up with just one story you can share with us from when you were young?"

"Okay," said the Master, "I will try."

A minute passed. The students sat in silence as the Master pondered.

"Ah, here is one for you," began the Master. "When I was about eight years old, my whole family was invited to attend a wedding in the village. The wedding celebration went on for three days. Oh, the people were so joyful and the ladies wore their boldest and most colorful festive garbs. And the food. It was plentiful. And always there was a generous supply of varied sweets to enjoy.

"My two brothers, Twan and Tikii, and I just could not let up on the sweets. We started into them on the first day, having to taste every different one. On the second day, we knew which were our favorites and loaded up on them. By the third day of the celebration, we were well aware there wouldn't be any more free sweets after that day, so we ate, and ate, and ate until all three of us turned green in the face and had to lay down because our stomachs ached so much. Two days later, we were still feeling sick."

The Master paused and looked long at his students. "Okay," he finally asked, "why do you think I shared this story with you? What lesson do you think I was able to learn from it that now you can learn too?"

"Just because sweets are abundant and free, it doesn't mean you have to overeat them," said Tonga.

"That's true," said the Master. "Anyone else?"

Leela piped up: "Don't eat sweets."

"Well, is that realistic, Leela?" asked the Master. "Imagine going through life without tasting and enjoying sweets."

Said Bizah, "I know that life would not be as sweet without sweets, Master. I guess the lesson here is: everything in moderation, including sweets. You, Master, would probably agree and say, 'Unless it is absolutely required, yes, everything in moderation'."

"I have nothing more to add," said the Master.

A true spiritual master knows
they will always remain a
student.

Tonga Impresses Bizah

It was the end of a long week of meditation and study. The Master called the students together and said he was going to give them a quiz.

"Now, why would I want to give you a quiz?" asked the Master.

"To find out how much we have learned," one student piped up.

"No," Tonga responded, "to find out how much more we still need to learn."

The Master nodded his head and gave Tonga a smile of deep approval.

Bizah nudged Leela, leaned over, and whispered in her ear: "That Tonga is really coming along."

A Long Day's Excursion

It was one of those sunny days when the Master decided that his students needed some fresh air, to be in nature, and to get some exercise. The group set off early in the morning for a hike. The students walked together as an organic, moving community led by the Master who was about ten paces ahead.

On and on they walked, taking a break only for lunch. As the sun was starting to fall, they knew their day of trekking was soon to be over. But just then, they came to a very steep hill that seemed to go on for a mile.

"Oh, Master, I'm so tired," sighed Bizah. "I don't think I can make it up that steep hill."

"Yes, you can," responded the Master. "If I as an old man can make it up that hill, then you certainly should be able to as well. Here is what I suggest you do. Forget about the hill being there. Don't look up as you walk, seeing only how much longer the climb will be. Keep your head down and attentive to just the one step you are taking in the present moment. The steep hill will disappear and you will see only the one step you are taking and needing to take at that time. In this way, you will be up at the top without thinking about the climb."

@BizahSays

If you are going to judge
something, judge results.

On Not Worrying About Others

Bizah awoke one morning quite disturbed. He was worrying about some of the Master's new students who were not disciplined in spiritual terms and whom he felt would soon have to leave the Master and be without his guidance because of their inability to learn the new ways.

As soon as Bizah spotted his Master alone in the garden, he approached him with this concern.

"Master," he said with an anguished tone, "what will become of the students you will have to ask to leave your presence because they are not ready to learn?"

The Master nodded to Bizah, acknowledging his concern, then said, "Bizah, don't worry. They are not lost. They will just have to come back again later."

On Understanding Angry Criticism

Bizah was particularly quiet one day. Noticing this, the Master went up to him and asked, "Is anything bothering you, Bizah?"

"Well, to be honest, yes Master. When I was down at the lake fishing a few days ago, there was another boy fishing there too. We started talking and it led to his asking me why I wore a robe all the time. I told him that I was a student of Truth and then started to explain what that meant. When I finished speaking, this boy – named Beeta, if I remember correctly – got really angry with me. He told me I was just stupid to devote myself to studying about Consciousness. He said I would not make it in the real world and that the spiritual path I was on would lead to nowhere. Master, I just can't understand why he got so very angry about my spiritual way."

"Bizah, you are still young," said his Master. "You will likely meet many people like this during your lifetime. The reason they get so angry is that your spiritual way challenges the belief system they have chosen. Because they identify who and what they are with the beliefs and doctrines of their chosen way, they feel threatened by others who have chosen another way.

"For Beeta to have opened to an understanding and acceptance that there was another way besides his own would have felt like a kind of death to him. He feels that in order to be safe in the world, he needs to hold onto his way. Anything or anyone other than what he believes to be true is seen as a threat to him—as an enemy.

"So you see, Bizah, Beeta was really afraid of you. He was threatened by what you shared with him about consciousness and he showed his fear through anger. Your not reacting to his anger with defensiveness or retaliation was a good thing."

Be excessively kind to others;
you never know the weight of
the hidden burdens they carry.

Service

"Master, I so very much want to serve others," Bizah said.

"That's good," said the Master. "But tell me why you want to be of service to others."

"Because I have so much love and compassion for my brothers and sisters that I can't contain it. It just bursts out."

"That's good. And how will you serve them?"

"By loving them in the most appropriate way I can."

"That's very good, Bizah."

The Myth of the Man In the Mask

"Have you heard the myth of the man in the mask?" asked Bizah.

"No," replied Akina. "What's it about?"

"Well, it goes like this: One day very long ago in human history, when we knew who we really were – divine and perfect – one man in his playfulness decided to trick a friend by putting on a face mask that expressed fear. It worked. His friend, looking at him in the mask, felt vulnerable and quickly walked away.

"The trickster was delighted that he could have such an effect on another simply by putting on a mask. It was great fun! So he tried again. This time, his mask caused the person to weep.

"Even more delighted because his trick had worked a second time, he tried it again, choosing to wear a mask of rage. Well, this evoked an even more powerful response in the person who next looked upon him, causing this person to run away in terror.

"The trickster was having so much fun at this game that he kept trying on different masks to get different reactions from others, until one day he couldn't take the mask off. He had become a combination of all the masks he had worn. And since that day, he has been trying to get back to his real face, his real nature."

"Hmm," said Akina. "Do you think this is what happened to all of us?"

"Don't know," responded Bizah. "This myth has lived for a long, long time, so there must be some truth in it."

@BizahSays

Appreciation and praise
are alchemical: they create
abundance.

Too Much of a Good Thing?

Bizah was walking with his Master in the garden. The sun was shining, and the weather was perfect. Both of them were silent as they took in the awesome beauty around them: the lush trees, the glorious flowers, the colorful wild birds, the blanket of verdant lawn under their feet. Every few minutes, Bizah couldn't help but express a deep sigh of gratitude. Eventually, however, he broke the shared silence with a question.

"Master, can one ever get too much of a good thing?"

"Only when one is not fully satisfied with the good thing he is presently blessed with experiencing."

Bizah Learns About Gratitude

Bizah was in the temple fingering through his long string of beads. Every day, he came in the early afternoon to give thanks. He would note something for which he was grateful, then go on to the next bead and do the same.

One day, he spent an extraordinarily long time in the temple, so his Master came looking for him.

"Bizah, you have been in here for over an hour giving thanks," said the Master. "What is taking you so long?"

"Master," said Bizah, "it is really hard for me today to find enough things to give thanks for. I really have to think about it."

"Bizah, when you are truly grateful for something, you don't have to think about it or go searching to identify it. Gratitude cannot be pulled from you. Gratitude is something that jumps from your heart and forces outward expression."

The Master continued: "Tonga spent only two minutes in the temple today expressing his gratitude. Those two minutes giving spontaneous thanks are more meaningful and powerful than more than the hour you spent thinking up things to be grateful for."

"If we have to look for things to be grateful for, it is

not gratitude: it is memory. Gratitude always surfaces spontaneously in the Now."

We can only lose what we identify with. Our true self cannot be robbed or deprived, since it only contains and will always contain everything of lasting value.

Bizah and the Thief

Bizah woke up with a start, as he heard his Master crying out, "Stop thief!"

He quickly got up and ran to see what he could do. But when he got to his Master's hut, the thief had already made his escape.

"Oh, Master," Bizah said, "you had so little and the thief had to take even that."

"Well, he really was a foolish thief," his Master responded. Then he pointed out of his window to his apple tree and said, "He took only dead objects and left the delicious life-giving fruit behind."

Watching Eagles Fly

"Master, I can lie here for hours just watching the eagles glide and swirl overhead. Why do I find them so intriguing, so absolutely engaging to watch?" asked Bizah.

"Bizah, the eagles are doing what is their nature to do, which is why they do it so beautifully. They fly, soar, glide easily and effortlessly. When we observe living forms – flowers, kittens, dolphins, children, and the like expressing so freely and joyfully their true nature, we are delighted. We are also intrigued because they remind us of what it is like to live from our true nature. Many of us have forgotten what that feels like."

Any negative emotion such as fear, jealosy, or anger brings with it an opportunity to be free of it.

Verbal Battling

"Master" said Bizah. "Yesterday Akina and I got into a terrible argument about which of your teachings was the most important. I thought it was to drop ego and Akina thought it was to trust that the force that runs the Universe is benign, is always wanting our greatest good.

"I got so angry at Akina. I yelled at him, I called him names, and I even wanted to punch him in the face because he couldn't see things my way. Today I feel awful about that. Master, why did I get into such a state?"

"Well, Bizah," the Master replied, "it is because you identified yourself with the mental position you took, and when it was threatened by Akina's strong arguments, you took that to actually be an attack on who you were. That's why you wanted to fight back so hard – to defend yourself, or who you think yourself to be.

"You are not the mental concepts you hold. You know this on a mental level but not yet on the deep level of self-awareness. When you come to truly realize who you are in your essence, you will no longer enter verbal arguments. Come back and tell me when this is so."

Disguise Is Disquieting After Awhile

"Bizah, I heard that you and the others went to a costume party last night to celebrate the coming of the harvest," said the Master.

"Yes," replied Bizah. "I went as a donkey, Leela as a milkmaid, and Tonga as a prince. It was a lot of fun to laugh at everyone else pretending to be someone they weren't. I'm sure my donkey costume caused a lot of people to laugh too. And I must say that my 'hee haws' sounded quite authentic. I found myself getting very tired by the end of the evening, however. Master, it takes a lot of energy to pretend you are something else."

"It does indeed, Bizah. Have you ever noticed that most humans are tired most of the time? It's because they too are pretending they are someone they are not. They are pretending they are limited and separate beings who need to struggle and compete against others to survive. Now, wouldn't that be an exhausting thing? Hopefully soon they will wake up and recognize they are not who they pretend they are and will claim their divine, unlimited true Self."

"Somehow, Master, I think you are also talking about me here, right?"

"If you feel I am, then I must be, Bizah."

Mutual understanding leads to
mutual cooperation.

When Work Is Too Hard

Bizah and the other students were complaining about how hard their Master had been pushing them of late. They got together and decided someone had to tell the Master how they felt. But who should that person be?

Everyone was reluctant to approach the Master about this, so when no one volunteered for the task, they drew straws.

Alas, Bizah was the loser, so it was up to him.

The next day, just as their lesson time was coming to a close, Bizah stood up and bowed to his Master. Then he asked, "Master, may I tell you something?"

"Of course, Bizah."

"Master, we all feel you have been pushing us too hard in our lessons lately and expecting us to quickly learn things we find hard to grasp."

"Oh," replied the Master. "I didn't know this. Just as a student has an obligation to the Master, the Master has an obligation to his students. If I have been expecting too much of you, that is not good. You will not learn when you feel this way. Thank you for telling me. Now, go and play."

Giving and Receiving Part I

The Master told a story.

"One day, a father asked his son to go to the market and find out the going price for a whole pig, since he had fattened theirs up and would soon be able to offer it for sale. He gave his son an egg from the almost empty pantry for when he got hungry.

"The boy set out, only to soon come across a beggar sitting by the side of the road. He gave him his egg.

"The boy continued on his way and was soon accompanied by a lady going to market. She was animated, friendly, talkative. She had a whole basket full of eggs, and being of generous heart, gave the boy two eggs.

"Just a short time later the boy met an undernourished mother with an infant child clinging to her breast. He opened her hand and placed his two eggs there.

"Next he came upon a farmer returning from the market with a wagon laden with fruits, vegetables, and – eggs. The farmer, feeling generous because he had gotten his supplies at a very good price that day, offered the boy four eggs.

"At the market, the boy traded one egg for a piece of yonga molasses bread, conducted his inquiry regarding the going price for a fat pig, then set out for home.

"On his way back, the boy came across a woman who had fallen by the side of the road. She had tripped and broken her leg. The boy instinctively came to her rescue, carrying her back to her farm two fields away. In gratitude, the woman gave him her royal laying hen.

"At dusk the boy approached his home with three eggs and a royal laying hen. His father was ecstatic. 'I sent you off to the market with one egg, and now look at what you have returned with. How did this good fortune come upon you, my son?' he asked.

"'Well, father, I tried to give my egg away, but it kept coming back to me – and multiplied – until I even ended up with this laying hen.'

"From then on, the family feasted daily on fresh eggs."

"Okay," said the Master, "what can you learn from this story?"

"If you give, you will receive," Tonga piped up.

"If you give, you will receive more than you have given," added Leela.

"In order to give, you first have to be a good receiver," added Akina. "The boy first gratefully received the egg from his father. If he hadn't, he would have had nothing to give."

"Bizah, do you have something to add?" asked the Master.

"Not really," replied Bizah.

"Okay then students, let me leave you with this to consider: How can receiving at the same time be giving? And how can giving at the same time be receiving?"

Giving and Receiving – Part II
The Lesson Continues

As expected, one morning the Master brought up the questions he left his students with at the end of lessons the previous day: "How can receiving at the same time be giving? And how can giving at the same time be receiving?"

Then the Master said, "I left you with two questions yesterday. Does anyone want to present their response at this time?"

There was a long silent pause.

"Well, Master," Bizah responded. "Your questions go to the heart of why we are here studying with you. We truly do want to be of service to others, to give of the highest we can offer."

Bizah added, "When I give, I receive because it makes me happy that someone else will experience joy in what I have given them – be it a contented smile, a helping hand, compassionate understanding, or an egg."

Bizah paused, then after a few moments continued, "Now, the question of how can receiving be the same as giving seems to be a more difficult one. But not really, if one just reverses things. To receive gratefully gives the giver a gift."

Said the Master, "Bizah, can you go a little deeper and tell us again why genuine giving and receiving are the same thing?"

There followed another long silent pause.

"Master, I think when we genuinely give with gratitude for being able to give, and genuinely receive with gratitude, thereby making the giver happy at the same time, we come to experience that the giver and receiver are one. That is the joy, the illumination we experience when giving and receiving, receiving and giving – that we are One."

In hearing this, the Master sat down. He had no words to add. He folded his hands and smiled with the humble pride of a Master.

He was well pleased. He received the gift.

It's easy to identify the things we want. Knowing what we don't need requires self-awareness and wisdom.

On Saying "No" and Feeling Good About It

Bizah and Tonga were picking berries one day when Tonga asked Bizah if he ever felt it hard to say "no" to people.

"At first I did, Tonga, but not anymore," Bizah replied.

"How did this change for you?"

"I used to find it hard to turn down an invitation or let people know that I wanted to just be alone or didn't want to participate in what they wanted to do. When I didn't want to but went along with what others wanted anyway, afterwards I would feel sad, then angry with myself for giving in and doing what I really didn't want to do. Saying 'yes' when I really wanted to say 'no' was making me unhappy.

"But then the Master helped me realize that if I do anything with inner resistance, I'm not helping myself or others because I'm bringing the negative energy of resentment to others, which isn't fair to them and certainly takes its toll on my well-being. Now, knowing that saying 'no' when I mean 'no' hurts no one, it's easy for me to say it. Does that help you, Tonga?"

Kindness expressed is kindness experienced - so too with generosity, encouragement, and love.

Bizah Continues to Learn About Giving and Receiving

Bizah couldn't stop thinking about the magic and the power of giving and receiving.

If what we give to others actually comes back to us, then why not give what we most want to receive? And we can give so many things: not just money, or objects, or time, or the work of our body and mind, but qualities we hold most dear or feel most in need of, such as patience, understanding, and peace.

Bizah thought he would put this to the test. When he woke in the middle of the night feeling anxious about this or that, or nothing in particular, he decided to send out peace to those who came to mind. "Peace be with you," he continued to repeat.

It worked! When he did this, in no time at all he was feeling peaceful himself and fell back asleep.

If No Fish Bite?

"Yes, we find fishing so much fun, but what if we never ever caught a fish or came to find out that there were really no fish in the pond?" said Bizah. "We wouldn't enjoy it then, Akina."

"Well, we could still enjoy laughing and talking while we fished. We could even imagine we caught many fish –big ones– and share our imaginary stories with excitement. That could be fun," said Akina.

"So then, why are people so anxious about catching fish?" asked Bizah.

"Well, I would be anxious about catching them if I needed them to eat and feed my family," replied Akina. "That is a good reason to want to catch fish."

"I also would really want to catch fish if I thought I would feel better about myself or others would think more highly about me for catching many fish," Akina continued. "But that is all for ego gratification. The Master has already taught us about that."

"Oh, you made me realize, Akina, that I don't really want to fish, but just enjoy the outdoors and share experiences with my good friend. Why don't we give our rods to some people who need to fish in order to eat?"

"Sounds good to me," responded Akina.

The ultimate trust is to trust
that Life has our best interests
at heart.

Bizah and His Master

"Bizah, after these years with me, what is the most important thing you have learned?" asked his Master.

"To be grateful that I have had these years with you, Master."

"Very good," responded the Master with a smile on his face.

Life Interrupted

The Master was moved at that instant to look out the small window in his hut, whereby he saw Bizah receive a letter from the village post person, read it, then go white in his face. Bizah dropped the note to the ground, then fell to the ground holding his head while crying and breathing in convulsions.

He was in deep despair.

The Master knew he should not run to Bizah at this time, but wait for Bizah to come to him.

The next morning, very early, Bizah came to the Master's abode and tapped on his door. The tap was hardly audible, but since the Master was awaiting such a thing, he was wide awake and heard it instantly.

The Master went to the door.

"Bizah, what do you have to tell me?"

"I received news that my mother has taken seriously ill, and because she has no one to look after her, I must go and care for her. But, Master, how can I leave you and my studies? How can I leave those who are so close to my heart and a part of my love of life: Akina, Tonga, Leela, and the others?"

"Bizah, life has called you to experience and learn in a different way at this time. And you are ready for it, my beloved student. Life is our teacher, no matter if it teaches us through others, through books, or through experiences – both joyful and painful."

"You are so right in knowing immediately that you must go to take care of your mother, Bizah," continued the Master. "When your mother is well again, or if she dies, you will return to us and teach us of all you have learned through this life experience. It may be the very thing that life is gifting you with to become a Master."

The Master in a rare show of outward affection, hugged Bizah to his heart – for a long, long while.

There's always more Bizah!

@BizahSays

The Birth of Bizah

Bizah, a student of Truth, showed up on a sunny day in August some years ago.

I was on vacation with my family in Naramata, a small community in the interior region of British Columbia, Canada. We were staying in a home on Lake Okanagan, where we were surrounded by stillness and abundant natural beauty. I took my laptop with me, just in case I was inspired to do some writing.

Toward the end of the second week of vacation, it felt like a book wanted to be birthed. When I started writing, the words poured out of me, the general content organizing itself quickly into chapters. This became the basis for what, years later, would be published as *The HOW to Inner Peace*.

As I was writing, Bizah suddenly showed up and wanted his own turn to speak. I was surprised and did not know where he came from! I tried not to question this and let what he had to say come through. In less than an hour, I had captured ten of Bizah's stories!

Once I had given him a voice, Bizah became an ever-present source of wisdom and inspiration to me. As I experienced different life events, Bizah told me what they meant and what I could learn from them. When he wanted to help me make sense of perplexing issues, he shared an appropriate story with me or a pithy statement of Truth. He prompted me to re-read certain Zen stories.

Each day – and often many times a day – he took me deeper into his world - a world of innocence and insight. I met his Master and his friends, and the sweet and playful stories kept finding their way onto the page. Quite quickly, and with very little effort, I had an entire book of stories to share.

Bizah's wisdom is ancient yet timely. He has the gift of reaching across religious, cultural, and geographical boundaries. He speaks to us all because we are all, like Bizah, just trying to find our way in the world, to become a better person, and do our best in service to others.

I am sharing these stories with you so that you too can have Bizah in your life - because it's so much better when he's around!

Namasté,

Constance Kellough

Constance Kellough - Author

Constance Kellough is Founder and Publisher of Namaste Publishing, Founder and Meditation Teacher at Innerbody Meditation and author of two additional books: *The Leap: Are You Ready to Live a New Reality?* (no longer in print) and *The HOW to Inner Peace* (published 2021).

Constance is a visionary who popularized the self-help genre, bringing evolutionary, spiritual teachings to the forefront of modern culture. Her first publication, *The Power of Now* introduced Eckhart Tolle to the world. Since 1997, she has gone on to publish more groundbreaking, inspirational books by such authors as Dr. Shefali Tsabary, Michael Brown and Dr. David Berceli. These books and many others have changed the dialogue around Spirituality, Conscious Parenting and Trauma Release practices worldwide.

Constance lives with her husband in Vancouver, BC, Canada, where she continues to write, publish inspirational books and teach meditation. *The Chronicles of Bizah, A Student of Truth* is her first work of fiction.

Mary Kellough - Illustrator

Mary Kellough is a Graphic and Interior Designer, Content Creator and Marketing Strategist. She has contributed to Namaste Publishing since its inception, playing key roles in Administration, Editorial, Creative and Production. She lives on an orchard in the birthplace of Bizah - Naramata, BC, Canada - with her family and two dogs, Dharma and Jeera.

The Chronicles of Bizah, A Student of Truth is her first illustrated book.

books that change your life

namaste
PUBLISHING

Our Publishing Mission is to make available healing
and transformational publications that acknowledge,
celebrate, and encourage our readers to live from their
true essence and thereby come to remember
who they truly are.

STAY INSPIRED.

WWW.NAMASTEPUBLISHING.COM

@NAMASTEBOOKS